discover Object Talks that teach about God

SUSAN L. LINGO

Standard®
PUBLISHING
Bringing The Word to Life
Cincinnati, Ohio

DEDICATION

But seek first his kingdom and his righteousness,
and all these things will be given to you as well.
Matthew 6:33

Discover-n-Do Object Talks That Teach About God
© 2002 by Susan L. Lingo

Published by Standard Publishing, Cincinnati, Ohio
wwww.standardpub.com

Credits
Produced by Susan L. Lingo, Bright Ideas Books™
Illustrated by Paula Becker
Cover design by Joel Armstrong

09 08 07   8 7 6

ISBN-13: 978-0-7847-1371-6
ISBN-10: 0-7847-1371-5

CONTENTS

INTRODUCTION

What would you do if you saw ...
  ✔ **Coins that disappear?**
    ✔ **Balloons that don't pop with pins?**
      ✔ **Bananas sliced inside the peels?**
        ✔ **Water that pours from rocks?**

What would you do? Why, you'd probably race to discover how it was done! And while you were making those exciting discoveries, you'd discover some amazing Bible truths, too! That's what *Discover-n-Do Object Talks That Teach About God* is all about. These object talks are different from other ho-hum chats. Here are twenty-three unique, eye-popping presentations and mighty messages that drive home important Bible truths and God's Word. Just think how excited your kids will be to see water coming from rocks as they discover the importance of obeying God, or how tickled they'll be seeing three coins turn into six as they discover how God multiplies our blessings when we share. These are eye-popping object talks that inspire heart-warming responses to God's Word! But wait ... are these cool demonstrations, memorable messages, and slick tricks easy enough for any teacher to prepare and present? Yes! Simple supplies and clear-cut directions are provided and guarantee to turn any teacher into an object-talk pro while grabbing kids' attention in unique and memorable ways!

Each object talk opens with a case to be solved, such as "Is there really power in prayer?" Then following every slick trick or powerful presentation, kids will collect clues to solve the case by reading the Bible and discovering the answers God gives us through his Word. Brief discussions and fun extra-time activities round out the object talks and provide meaningful, memorable fun for kids of all ages!

So what are you waiting for? Grab your sleuth's hat and magnifying glass, put on your gumshoes, and lead kids in discovering the power in God's Word with *Discover-n-Do Object Talks That Teach About God!* Be sure to look for the other Discover-n-Do Object Talks books in the series: *Discover-n-Do Object Talks That Teach About Jesus* and *Discover-n-Do Object Talks That Teach About the Holy Spirit!*

POWERED & POSSIBLE

Matthew 19:26; Mark 10:27; Luke 18:27; Philippians 4:13

The Clue: *How does God helps us accomplish the "impossible"?*

Simple Supplies: You'll need a Bible, several raw potatoes, sturdy plastic drinking straws, newsprint, markers, and tape.

A day prior to class, practice this slick trick several times with a different potato than the one you'll use in class. This trick will impress your kids in class as well as dinner guests! The object is to thrust the plastic straw cleanly through the center of the uncooked potato. To do this, hold the potato in one hand and with a quick, powerful motion, thrust the straw at an angle down through the potato. (Wow! It really can be done!) What a neat way to use potatoes and remind others that nothing is impossible with God's power!

Discover 'n Do!

Hold a raw potato in one hand and a plastic straw in the other. Challenge kids to see if they can push the straw through the potato. (Since they don't know the secret to the trick, they won't be able to impale the potato.) Say: **Wow! This seems like an impossible feat to accomplish, doesn't it? There are many times in life when we think something is impossible or a situation is unconquerable. When have you felt as if something was impossible?** Encourage kids to share their experiences and feelings, then continue by reading aloud Luke 18:27. Say: **We might feel that some things are hopeless, but the Bible tells us that nothing is impossible with God, if we have faith in God's power.** Thrust the straw through the potato and wait for kids' excited reactions. Then say: **Nothing is impossible for God. But how does he help us accomplish the impossible? How does God empower us to conquer the unconquerable? Let's see if we can solve the case with a little detective work and the Bible!**

Collect the Clues!

Have small groups of kids look up and read the following verses: Matthew 19:26; Mark 10:27; and Philippians 4:13. Challenge kids to decide how God uses his power to help us. Then tape a sheet of newsprint to the wall and have kids read their verses aloud and list the ways God helps us accomplish the "impossible," such as through prayer, his Word, faith, and God's miracles. Then ask:

✔ How does faith help us accomplish God's plans?

✔ In what ways can prayer be a powerful help in accomplishing what seems hopeless?

✔ Why does God want us to trust his power and remain hopeful?

Show kids how the potato trick is done, then say: **What seems impossible may not be impossible. God gives us the ways and means to accomplish even the most hopeless or impossible feats. We just need to follow his directions!** Close by saying: **Good for you—you've solved the clues! It's through God's power, our faith, and prayer that the impossible becomes possible. This case is closed!**

If there's time, invite kids to make raw-potato prints on newsprint and blow drops of tempera paint around their papers with the drinking straws. Title the colorful creations: "All things are possible with God!"

H EY, NO PROBLEM!

Psalm 46:1; Proverbs 2:6, 12; Daniel 2:20; Romans 11:33

The Case: *How does God help us solve problems?*

Simple Supplies: You'll need a Bible, a pitcher of water, a clear glass tumbler, several pennies, index cards, a dish pan, and markers.

Before class time, you'll want to try out this cool trick—by the sink! Drop a few pennies in a clear glass tumbler filled three-fourths full of water. Place an index card over the top of the tumbler and hold it tightly against the top using your flattened palm. Quickly turn the tumbler over and place it on a table or counter. Slide the card out from the cup. Wipe up any drips. The idea is to figure out how to get the coins from under the glass without spilling the water all over the table! It's really quite easy: Simply slide the tumbler to the edge of the table and, holding the dish pan under the edge, let the water empty into the pan. (You'll set the pan aside during the demonstration so kids won't see it!) If you plan for extra time, collect a drinking glass for each child to decorate with stained-glass paints.

Discover 'n Do!

Shortly before the object talk, prepare the coins under the glass of water. Place the dish pan out of sight near you. Gather kids around the "problem

6

coins" and say: **Wow! Now here's a real dilemma! I want to get these coins out from under the glass, but I don't want to spill any water on the table or floor. How can I solve this problem?** Let kids discuss their ideas and brainstorm a few possible solutions if they can. Then say: **We all face many problems during our lives. Some of those problems are small and easily solved.** Show kids how to remove the coins using the dish pan. Then continue: **Some problems are big dilemmas and require extra-special help to be solved or overcome. What are problems you've faced and needed help solving?** Encourage kids to share their experiences, then say: **When problems are big and scary, it's good to turn to someone who can help!**

Read aloud Psalm 46:1, then say: **Isn't it great knowing that God can always help us solve dilemmas? When we ask for God's help, he provides special tools we can use in solving problems.** Pull out the dish pan and retrieve the coins. **How does God help us solve problems? Let's see if we can solve this case with a little detective work and the Bible!**

Collect the Clues!

Hand each child an index card and a marker. Challenge kids to write on the index cards one problem they need help in solving. Then have volunteers read aloud Psalms 31:16; 46:1; Proverbs 2:6, 12; Daniel 2:20; Romans 11:33. Briefly discuss how each verse provides a way to solve the problems written on the cards. Then ask:

✔ **How does learning God's Word help us discover ways to solve problems?**

✔ **In what ways does God send others to help us?**

✔ **Why is it important to ask God for help through prayers?**

✔ **Why is having patience while waiting on God's answers important?**

Let kids practice putting the coins in the tumbler and removing them using the dish pan. Challenge kids to demonstrate this object talk to their families and friends as they remind them of God's power to help us solve problems. Then have kids place their "problem cards" in the empty tumbler. Say: **When we give our problems to God and ask for his help in solving them, God gives us patience, wisdom, trust, and other**

people to help us overcome our problems and troubles. Good for you—you've solved the clues. This case is closed!

If there's time, let kids use stained-glass paints to decorate glass tumblers to use as "problem-catchers." Tell kids to write any worries or problems they have on slips of paper and place them in the tumblers as they ask God for help and use patience as they wait for his answers.

⊕OD'S X-RAY VISION

1 Samuel 2:3; Psalm 44:21; Luke 16:15; 1 John 3:20

The Case: *Who sees inside our hearts and knows our thoughts?*

Simple Supplies: You'll need a Bible, a paper sack, sturdy party tooth-picks, a banana for each child plus one extra, paper plates, and powdered fruit-flavored gelatin.

Before class, place all the items in the paper sack. When you choose bananas for this activity, choose bananas that have small brown speckles on the peels. Prepare a banana for the object talk by poking a toothpick through the peel and gently move the toothpick back and forth to slice through the banana inside the peel (see diagram). Repeat the "secret slicing" at one-inch intervals down the length of the banana. When the banana is peeled during the object talk, it will be "miraculously" sliced! Place the prepared banana in the paper sack but keep track of which banana it is!

Discover 'n Do!

Set the sack in front of kids and ask them to tell what they think is inside. After guesses are made, point out that an X-ray machine or X-ray vision could be really helpful to see the inside of the sack. Say: **Of course we don't have X-ray vision to see the insides of things or know what others are feeling or thinking, but God knows. It's almost as if God has divine X-ray vision!**

Read aloud 1 John 3:20, then pull the pre-sliced banana from the sack. Say: **Sometimes we think we know what a person is feeling or what**

they're like inside, just as we think we may know what this banana is like on the inside.

Have kids tell what they think the banana is like inside the peel, then ask a volunteer to come peel the banana over a paper plate. Say: **Wow! Most bananas get sliced after they're peeled, but this banana was sliced inside the peeling! We didn't really know what was inside, but God knew. God knows everything, including our thoughts, feelings, and what we're like inside our hearts and if we're kind or have mean attitudes. Let's discover more about what God knows and sees. We'll see if we can solve the case with a little detective work and the Bible!**

Collect the Clues!

Form four small groups and assign each group one of the following verses to read: 1 Samuel 2:3; Psalm 44:21; Luke 16:15; and Acts 15:8. Have kids read to discover clues as what to God sees or knows, then report their findings to the rest of the class. Then ask:

✔ **Why is it good that God knows everything?**

✔ **In what ways is God knowing our thoughts and feelings a demonstration of his love and care? his ultimate power?**

✔ **How does God's divine X-ray vision help us stay honest with God? with others?**

Say: **Let's have some fun learning how to pre-slice bananas in the peel so you can show your friends and families as you remind them about God's divine X-ray vision.**

Distribute bananas, toothpicks, and paper plates and demonstrate how to slice the bananas inside the peels. Invite kids to find partners and slice the bananas in the peels. Challenge kids to present the mini devotion about God's divine X-ray vision to each other as they peel the bananas over paper plates to reveal the slices. Sprinkle the banana slices with sparkly, fruit-flavored gelatin mix. Then invite kids to nibble their party bananas using toothpicks as "picker-uppers" as they discuss ways God helps us by knowing all things. Share a prayer thanking God for his divine vision, then close by saying: **Good for you—you've solved the clues! Only God sees our hearts and knows all our thoughts. The case is closed!**

WHATTA NAME! ow April 2010

Exodus 9:16; 20:7; Psalms 20:1, 5; 68:4; Jeremiah 10:6

The Case: *What power is in God's name?*

Simple Supplies: You'll need a Bible, markers, white paper, and a paper lunch sack. (If you plan to do the extra activity, you'll also need thick tempera paints, brushes, glitter, and white construction paper.)

Before class, tear a piece of white paper into three rows, then tear each row into three squares. You should have nine squares. Notice that only one square will have all four edges ragged—this is the square you'll be focusing on and picking out during object-talk time. The idea will be to have nine kids secretly write their favorite names on the squares of paper, then place the papers in a paper sack. (Remember who had the square with the four ragged edges!. Let's say it was "Lindsay" for our example.) You'll then pull the squares from the sack and wow the kids by telling which was Lindsay's favorite name! Plan to tear a new sheet of paper with the kids. Write the phrase "El Elyon" on one sheet of paper and the following verse references on another: Psalm 20:1; Psalm 20:5; Psalm 68:4; Exodus 9:16; Exodus 20:7; and Jeremiah 10:6.

Discover 'n Do!

Have a sheet of white paper, markers, and a paper lunch sack beside you. Ask kids how they got their names, if they know. Then tell kids you'll have a little fun with favorite names and writing them on pieces of paper. Tear the sheet of paper into nine squares and distribute them with markers. (Remember who receives the ragged-edged square!) Turn your back and have kids secretly write their favorite names on the papers. Then ask a volunteer to place the squares in the paper sack. As you shake the sack, say: **I'm going to read these favorite names, then I will pick out the favorite name of ...** (pause and say the name of the child who had the ragged-edged square). One by one, pull out the names and read them aloud. Then pause for effect before naming the child with the special square.

Say: **Wow! How did I know whose name this was? I'll share that secret in moment. But first, there were many favorite names in this sack—names that sound pretty, cool, fun, or popular. I know another name that is the most powerful, special name in the world!** Hold up the paper with the name "El Elyon" written on it. **This is the Hebrew name for God Most High. But why is God's name so special? What power is in God's name? Let's see if we can solve this case with a little detective work and the Bible!**

Collect the Clues!

Display the verses you listed on a sheet of paper and have kids form six small groups. Assign each group a different verse to look up and read. Have groups briefly discuss what they learn about God's name from the verses, then share their discoveries with the class. Here is a list of what each verse reveals about the power in God's name:

✔ *power to protect (Psalm 20:1)*
✔ *power to be praised and exalted (Psalm 68:4)*
✔ *power to be shared with others (Exodus 9:16)*
✔ *power to be used with respect (Exodus 20:7)*
✔ *power to be victorious (Psalm 20:5)*
✔ *power to be mighty (Jeremiah 10:6)*

After reading the verses aloud and sharing each group's discoveries, ask:
✔ **How can we put the power in God's name to work in our lives?**
✔ **In what ways does the power in God's name help us know God? know what he can do?**
✔ **How can we thank God for the incredible power in his name?**
Say: **There are so many names in the world, but none even come close to the power in God's name! Isn't it great to know that we serve a God who is all-powerful and whose name inspires protection, praise, and respect? Whatta name! Whatta a mighty God we serve!** If you'd like, sing "Awesome God," then show kids how you picked out the favorite name from the paper bag.

If there's time for a quick craft project, have kids fold construction paper in half and use thick tempera paint write to "El Elyon" just above the fold. Carefully fold the paper and gently rub to transfer the paint and make a mirror image of the name. Open the paper and sprinkle glitter on the wet paint. When the papers are dry, kids can hang their name prints on their walls as reminders of the power in God's special name. Close by saying: **Good for you—you've solved the clues! There's power to praise, protect, trust, give thanks, and help in God's perfect name. This case is closed!**

⊕IDDEN WORD

Psalm 119:105; Proverbs 30:5; Isaiah 40:8; Ephesians 6:17

The Case: *What does God's Word do for us?*

Simple Supplies: You'll need a Bible, paper lunch sacks, markers, red construction paper, tape, scissors, and copies of the verse cards from this activity (page 13).

Before class, you'll need to prepare a lunch sack with a secret flap. To do this, you'll need two paper lunch sacks. Cut the bottom and narrow side from one sack and position it over the bottom and narrow side of the other sack matching the edges carefully. You want it to seem as if the inserted piece is really the inside of the new sack. Tape the edges of the bottom piece in place but leave the side untaped so it moves back and forth to create a hidden flap. This will be where you'll hide verse cards before the object talk. Kids will see an "empty" sack, then you'll amazingly pull cards from the sack! Copy the verse cards and cut them apart. Slide the cards in the hidden flap. (Be sure to hold the edge of the hidden flap tightly against the sack during the presentation so the cards won't escape before it's time!) Cut out a red paper heart and tape it to the front of the sack.

Discover 'n Do!

Be sure the verse cards are hidden in the paper sack. Show kids the sack and ask them to guess what might be inside. Then show them the "empty" inside of the sack (hold the flap edge securely closed). Say: **This paper sack represents our hearts and what might be inside. This poor heart appears to be empty, but there is something of great value hidden inside—something God tells us to hide in our hearts. What does God want us to hide in our hearts, and how can this hidden treasure help us? Let's see if we can solve the case with a little detective work!**

Collect the Clues!

Show kids the empty inside of the sack once more, then reach inside and slyly pull out a verse card. Hand the card to a volunteer to read aloud.

Briefly discuss what each card teaches us about what's to be hidden in our hearts before pulling out another card. When all the cards have been revealed, ask:

✔ **What's to be hidden in our hearts?**
✔ **What great things does God's Word do for us?**
✔ **In what ways does God's Word draw us closer to God? help us obey him?**
✔ **How can we hide the Word in our hearts?**

Read aloud Psalm 119:105, then say: **God knows his Word is perfect, true, and stands forever. God also knows his Word helps us obey him and live our lives as God desires. When we know what God says to us, we can put his powerful Word to work in our lives.**

Show kids how you did this cool trick, then if there's time, let kids make their own hidden-in-our-hearts sacks to show others. Make extra copies of the verse cards and have kids write Psalm 119:105 on the hearts taped to their sacks. Close by saying: **Good for you—you've solved the clues to this important case! God's Word is to be hidden in our hearts and used to obey God and draw us closer to him. This case is closed!**

"Your word is a lamp to my feet and a light
for my path." (Psalm 119:105)

"Every word of God is flawless."
(Proverbs 30:5)

"The word of our God stands forever."
(Isaiah 40:8)

"Your word is truth."
(John 17:17)

"Take the helmet of salvation and the sword of the
Spirit, which is the word of God." (Ephesians 6:17)

⬤UPER SAVER

Psalms 6:4; 7:10; 55:16; 109:26; 116:5; Isaiah 12:2

The Case: *How does God cover and protect us?*

Simple Supplies: You'll need a Bible, a package of balloons, clear tape, straight pins, and permanent markers.

Prior to class, blow up a balloon and tie the end. Place a piece of tape somewhere on the side of the balloon. If you slowly stick a straight pin through the center of the tape, the balloon won't pop! (Neat, isn't it?) Since kids cannot see the clear tape, they'll be amazed when it looks as if you've stabbed a balloon with a sharp pin and it doesn't explode. Be sure to have a balloon ready with the tape in place before class, but don't forget where on the balloon you placed the tape! You'll need two balloons for each child plus additional straight pins and tape if you'd like kids to try this slick trick themselves.

Discover 'n Do!

Draw a simple face on the balloon (beside the tape!) and add a small frown. Have the permanent marker and straight pin beside you. Hold the balloon and say: **Let's pretend this balloon is a friend. Why do you think he's frowning or looking a bit unhappy?** Suggest to the kids that the balloon friend is having a tough day, just as we sometimes have.

Say: **Just like all people, our balloon friend has worries and troubles that poke at him from time to time.** Hold up the straight pin. **Sometimes our worries and troubles can build up until we feel like popping or exploding!** Threaten to pop the balloon by moving the straight pin close, but don't pop it. (Be sure that you have the tape located!) **But our balloon friend has a secret weapon to keep him from popping from pressures and troubles! See? When troubles poke** (push the pin through the center of the tape), **our friend stays together!** Turn the balloon's frown into a smile using the marker. **What turns our friend's frown upside down and into a smile even in tough times? Let's see if we can solve the case with a little detective work and the Bible!**

Collect the Clues!

Have kids form six small groups and assign each group one of the following verses from Psalms to read and discuss: 6:4; 7:10; 55:16; 109:26; and

116:5. Have kids decide why God saves and helps us and how God shows his love through saving us. After a few minutes, invite each group to share their verse and discoveries. Then ask:

- ✔ **In what ways does trusting God's help save us from more worry?**
- ✔ **Why is it wise to trust in God's saving grace and help?**
- ✔ **In what ways can we thank God for his protection, help, and love?**

Say: **God knows that life holds many disappointments, troubles, and worries. But God doesn't leave us without hope or help. God covers us with love and compassion so that during times of trouble, we can rely on his help. God never gives us more than we can handle, and he's always there to keep us from popping under pressure!** Hold up the happy balloon. **Just as our pretend friend is smiling, we'll keep smiling when we trust in God's help.**

Read aloud Isaiah 12:2, then close by saying: **Good for you—you've solved the clues! God keeps us from "popping" under pressure by saving us, helping us, giving us hope, and covering us with his love. This case is closed!**

If there's time, hand each child a balloon to blow up and tie off. Show kids how to place a small piece of tape on their balloons and how to gently poke the pin through the center of the tape to keep the balloon from exploding. Then let kids blow up another balloon and write: "I will trust in God!" on the balloons using permanent markers. Have kids affix tape to their balloon and hand each child a straight pin to take home. Challenge kids to present the object talk to their families as they remind them of God's protective help and love.

F LIP FOR HOPE

Psalms 25:5; 31:24; 33:20, 22; 65:5, 6

The Case: *How does hope keep us strong and steady?*

Simple Supplies: You'll need a Bible, white copy paper, and markers. (If you want to really wow your kids, use a 5-foot length of white shelf paper instead of white copy paper. You'll still need the copy paper for kids.)

Before class, practice folding and unfolding the paper for this neat object talk—kids will flip for it! First, draw a happy face of yourself on the paper, then follow the folding instructions in the margin. Fold the paper downward, then fold to the right, then fold the back to the front, and unfold the paper upward to open it. The face should now be upside down. Fold the paper again in the same

way, and the face will flip right-side up. (Neat, isn't it?) If you plan to use a huge piece of paper, you may want to draw your entire self and not just your face. Be sure to practice folding and unfolding for smoothness during your presentation! Have paper and markers ready for kids to use.

Discover 'n Do!

Have the paper with the face or figure drawn on it handy. Ask kids to tell about times they might have felt hopeless or frustrated. Encourage kids to tell how it feels to be hopeless. Hold up the happy face and say: **Most days, we feel happy and can face life's little bumps.** (Begin folding the paper as you continue.) **But there are other times when sadness, frustrations, hurt feelings, or illness can make us feel hopeless and helpless. These feelings can really turn us upside down and keep us from serving God with cheerful hearts.** Unfold the paper to reveal the upside-down face. Then begin the reverse folding, and say: **We need to hold on to hope to stay happy and keep our faith upright!** Unfold the paper to reveal the right-side up smiling face. **But how can we keep hold of hope in hard times, and how does having hope help us stay strong and full of faith? Let's see if we can solve this case with a little detective work and the Bible!**

Collect the Clues!

Form five groups and assign each group one of these verses from Psalms to look up and read: 25:5; 31:24; 33:20; 33:22; 65:5, 6. Have kids read for clues as to who is our hope, what hope does for us, and how we can have hope. Then invite groups to read their verses aloud and share their thoughts and discoveries with the class. Ask:

✔ **Who is the only one we want to place our hope in? Explain.**
✔ **How does having hope strengthen us through tough times?**

✔ In what ways does obeying and trusting God give us hope?

✔ How does having hope help us serve God? serve others?

Say: **Feeling hopeless and helpless turns us upside down and robs us of faith and the joy to serve God and others. But obeying God, trusting him, resting in his love, and relying on God for strength gives us hope and turns our lives right-side up. When we have hope, we can stand strong and steady!**

Hand each child a sheet of white copy paper. Tell kids to use markers to draw their smiling faces on the papers. Then slowly demonstrate the folding and unfolding directions so kids can flip the faces upside down and right-side up again. Finally, have kids write Psalm 31:24 on the backs of their papers: "Be strong and take heart, all you who hope in the LORD." Then challenge kids to show this cool paper-flip trick to their families and friends as they remind others about placing our hope in God.

Close by saying: **Good for you—you've solved the clues! God is the only place to put our hope that strengthens, saves, and supports us. This case is closed!**

RUTH TRACKER

Psalms 26:3; 33:4; 43:3; Proverbs 17:24; John 17:17

The Case: *How can we discern truth from deceit?*

Simple Supplies: You'll need a Bible, marker, tape, newsprint, and a deck of playing cards, Old Maid cards, or animal rummy cards. (You can also use a deck of index cards with stickers or smiley faces drawn on one side of each card.)

Before class, practice this simple illusion with a friend. Turn the deck of cards or index cards so that all the pictures face the same direction. Fan out the cards so they're face down, then invite a friend to pull a card from the deck and look at it. (As your friend views the card, slyly turn the deck of cards around.) Tell your friend to remember the card, then slide it into the deck without peeking at the card. (Here's the key: Be sure the card is upside down from the rest of the deck! This will make it easy to find later!) Then spread the cards in a face-down fan on the table and find the upside down card. You'll astound your friend with your amazing ability to choose the "right" among the "wrong"! Finally, cut a large letter T from newsprint or construction paper and tape it to a wall. Place a marker close by.

Discover 'n Do!

Be sure the cards in your deck are all facing the same direction, then say: **I have a deck of cards to help us discover an important Bible truth. Who would like to choose a card from this deck?** Invite the volunteer to choose a card and show it to the other kids without you peeking at it. As the card is being shown, slyly turn the deck around as you say: **We'll pretend that the card you see is the truth and the rest of the cards represent lies. Let's hide the truth among many lies and see what happens.** Have the volunteer slide the card into the deck. (Be sure the card is facing opposite from the rest of the deck! If you want an extra showy touch, carefully mix the cards being careful not to change the direction of the cards.)

Say: **In a world that's filled with lies, it's important to be able to pick out or discern the truth from the deceit. False words, false prophets, and phony advertising are all around us. Lies are meant to mislead us. When we want to follow God, we want to follow the truth and be able to find God's truth among the lies.** Fan the cards out face down until you can pick out the card the volunteer chose. Show kids the card and wait for the amazed responses. Then say: **You see? We can pick the truth from the lies if we know how! But how can we separate deceit from truth, and how does God help us accomplish this feat? Let's see if we can solve this case with a little detective work and the Bible!**

Collect the Clues!

Gather kids by the letter T on the wall. Explain that the T stands for the word *truth* and that you'll be listing ways to find the truth on this letter. Then read each of the following verses aloud and decide what the verse teaches us about how to find the truth: Psalms 26:3; 33:4; 43:3; Proverbs 17:24; and John 17:17. List ways to find the truth on the letter T. Ways might include obeying God, trusting God's Word, gaining wisdom, and allowing God to guide us. Then ask:

✔ **What harm is there in not knowing God's truth?**

✔ **How can discerning the truth from lies help us stay close to God?**

✔ **In what ways does knowing God's Word help us separate truth from lies?**

Show kids how you chose the correct card earlier, then invite several kids to try the trick. Challenge kids to present this object talk at home for their friends and families as they remind others about the importance of separating God's truth from the lies that surround us. If there's time, let kids make their own small decks of twenty cards by having them decorate index cards using markers. Have kids draw pictures that can be turned to face a common direction. Scenes and faces work well for one side of the cards, then draw geometric shapes on the other sides of the cards.

Close by saying: **Good for you—you've solved the clues! God's Word helps us separate the truth from lies. This case is closed!**

 H EY ... OBEY!

Numbers 20:8-11; Psalm 119:101; Luke 11:28

The Case: *Why is obeying God so important?*

Simple Supplies: You'll need a Bible, a small sponge, a medium-sized rock, water, a plastic funnel, scissors, a marker, and brown paper. If you plan to let kids make their own funnels, have a funnel for each child, sponges, rocks, scissors, and permanent markers.

Before class, prepare for and practice this awesome trick—kids will love this one! Cut a piece of sponge to fit inside a plastic funnel along one side (about 3-inches square). During the object talk, you'll be secretly holding the damp sponge against the inside edge of the funnel and squeezing it as a volunteer taps a rock held above the funnel. It will appear as if water is coming from the rock! The big hint: Don't let kids see the sponge before, during, or immediately after the presentation! It might help to sit at a table for this object talk and hide the sponge on your lap. Finally, cut a large rock

shape from brown construction paper or a paper grocery sack and label the rock "Rock-Solid Obedience." Tape the rock to the wall.

Discover 'n Do!

Just before the object talk, wet the sponge thoroughly (but not dripping wet) and keep it hidden from kids. Set the funnel and rock on a table. Say: **We all know what can happen if we disobey our teachers and parents—we get into trouble and may be punished. Moses discovered the same thing about obeying God. When God set the Israelites free from Egypt, they wandered in the wilderness and became very thirsty. God gave Moses important directions for how to call water from a rock and give God the thanks and glory for helping his people.** Hand the rock to a volunteer and quickly hold the damp sponge in place in the funnel.

Continue: **Moses obeyed God—almost. He held his wooden staff over the rock and struck the rock twice with his staff.** Have the volunteer tap the rock two times—as he does so, squeeze the sponge to release the water through the funnel. (Then quickly hide the sponge as the kids "ooo" and "ahh!") Say: **As Moses struck the rock, he called forth the water and it came from the rock just as God had promised. But Moses disobeyed God and took credit for the miraculous feat himself! Moses didn't give God the credit or the glory. Moses disobeyed God in a big way!**

And what happened then? God punished Moses by refusing to let him enter into the Promised Land with the rest of his people. In the end, Moses discovered a great deal about obeying God. But why is it important to obey God in all we do and say, and how can we obey him better? Let's see if we can solve this case with a little detective work and the Bible!

Collect the Clues!

Gather kids by the paper rock taped to the wall and have a marker ready. Read the following verses and discuss what each teaches us about the importance of obeying God and how we can obey him better: Deuteronomy 27:10; Psalms 103:20; 119:101; and Luke 11:28. List the ways to obey God on the paper rock. Suggestions might include reading the Bible, praying, listening to God, and praising and following him. Then ask:

✔ **Why is it wise to obey God?**

✔ **What might happen if we choose to disobey the Lord?**

✔ **How does obeying God keep us safe from harm? help us learn about trust?**

✔ **In what ways can we acknowledge God as our Leader and obey and follow him in every way?**

Show kids how you "called" water from the rock, and if there's time, let kids cut sponges and decorate plastic funnels to make their own water-from-the-rock props. Let kids practice the object talk with partners. Have kids show their families and friends this neat trick as they remind others about the importance of obeying God.

Close by saying: **Good for you—you've solved the clues! It's important to obey God to keep us safe, happy, healthy, and close to him. The case is closed!**

SHOW 'N TELL

Psalm 33:11; Romans 8:28; Philippians 2:13

The Case: *How does God reveal his plans for us?*

Simple Supplies: You'll need a Bible, a mirror, a bar of white soap, scissors, stapler, copies of the verse cards from page 48, and old building plans that can be cut apart. (Check with contractors or architects for old plans or make copies of building plans from a home-improvement book.)

Before class, try this slick trick on the bathroom mirror at home to see how it works. Use wet soap to write something on the mirror. When it dries and is blown on, the word will be revealed. For the object talk, write the word "hope" on a handheld mirror using a bar of wet soap and allow it to dry. Kids will blow on the mirror to reveal the hidden word. You'll also need to cut a 6-inch square from the blueprints or building plans for each child as well as make a copy of the verse boxes for each person.

Discover 'n Do!

Set the mirror aside and ask kids to tell what plans they have for the day or upcoming week. Encourage them to tell how it feels to have exciting plans to look forward to. Then say: **Did you know that God has plans for you? We may not know exactly what God has planned or what his will is, but we do know two things: one, that God will reveal his plans for us, and two, that God gives us something wonderful through showing us his plans. What is this wonderful thing? Let's see if it can be revealed through this mirror.** Pass the mirror around and have each person blow on it.

When the word "hope" is revealed, read the word aloud and say: **Wow! Hope is revealed when we know that God has plans for us! We can look forward to what God has planned for us and rest assured that his plans will be for good and will be accomplished. Now that's exciting news! But how does God reveal his plans and let us know what he wants us to do? Let's see if we can solve the case with a little detective work and the Bible!**

Collect the Clues!

Hand each child a square of blueprint paper. Explain that God's plans are much like building plans. He knows in advance what his purposes and plans are for us, and step by step he helps us work through his plans until they are accomplished. Distribute the verse cards and take turns reading them aloud and briefly discussing what each teaches us about trusting God's plans for us. Then ask:

✔ **How do we know God's plans for us are good?**
✔ **In what ways does the Bible help reveal God's purposes and plans?**
✔ **How can prayer help us see God's plans for our lives more clearly?**
✔ **In what ways does God reveal his plans through his eternal promises?**
✔ **Why is it good to hope in God's plans?**

Have kids cut apart the verse cards and assemble them into a booklet using the blueprints as covers. Staple the booklets together. Then show kids how to use soap on the mirror to write the word "hope." Tell kids to write this word on a mirror at home and let it dry, then have their families or friends reveal the word as they remind others about God's plans for us and how they're revealed.

Close by saying: **Good for you—you've solved the clues! God reveals his plans for us through prayer, his Word, and his promises. And God's plans give us hope for the future, too. The case is closed!**

# O HIDING!

Psalm 139:1-12; Hebrews 4:13

The Case: *Is it possible to hide from God?*

Simple Supplies: You'll need a Bible, three foam cups, a penny, a blonde hair, and invisible tape. If you plan on the extra-time activity, you'll also need tacky craft glue, a small box for each child, paper, markers, and craft scraps such as sequins, velvet, seashells, buttons, and other items to embellish the boxes.

Before class, prepare and practice this simple but simply awesome trick. Tape a blonde hair to a penny using invisible tape. Place the penny tape-side down on a table with two upside-down cups. Cover the penny with the third cup making sure the hair is sticking out from the cup just a "hair"!) You'll be playing the old-fashioned shell game and identifying the cup with the hidden coin much to the amazement of the kids. The big hint: Be careful not to tangle the hair under the cup when you move the cups around, and always place the penny tape-side down on the table.

Discover 'n Do!

Have the cups lined up on a table and hold the penny with the attached hair. Say: **I have an amazing ability to see hidden things and tell where something is hiding. I'll show you using this penny.** Show kids the penny, then place it tape-side down on the table. Cover the penny with a cup and move the cups around. Invite a volunteer to gently slide the cups as you look away and say: **I will now show you which cup is hiding the penny!**

Pretend to search and think a bit for effect as you look for the hair. Lift off the cup hiding the penny. Repeat the demonstration once more, then say: **That was pretty amazing, wasn't it? But we all know I can't really see all things that are hidden. I used a fun little trick to find the hidden coin, which I'll show you in a few minutes. That penny just couldn't hide from me, but is it possible for us to hide from God? Is** there anything he can't see or any place we can go to get away from God? Let's see if we can solve the case with a little detective work and the Bible!

Collect the Clues!

Ask several volunteers to take turns reading the verses in Psalm 139:1-12. Then ask:

✔ **Is there any place we can hide from God? Explain.**

✔ **Why is it nice to know that God is always with us and knows where we are?**

✔ **Can we hide any of our thoughts, feelings, or dreams from God? Explain.**

✔ **How does knowing that we can't hide from God in any way help us obey God and do as he desires?**

Read aloud Hebrews 4:13, then say: **Because God created the world and each of us, he loves and cares for us. And because God loves and cares for us, he stays with us and there is no place we can go to be without God. In other words, we can never hide from God—but then, who would ever want to? It makes me feel wonderful to know that God's powerful love is huge enough to keep such careful track of us!** Show kids how the hidden coin trick was done and challenge them to present this object talk at home as they remind their families that nothing is hidden from God's sight or love.

If there's time, let kids embellish small boxes with colorful craft scraps. Tell kids they may be able to place special treasures inside their treasure boxes and hide them from others, but just as God knows what's hidden in our hearts, he knows what's inside the treasure boxes. Have kids write Hebrews 4:13 on small squares of paper and slip them in their treasure boxes. Encourage them to hide Scripture verses in their treasure boxes.

Close by saying: **Good for you—you've solved the clues! Nothing and no one is hidden from God. He knows our thoughts and keeps perfect track of us. This case is closed!**

CHOSEN ONES

Colossians 3:12; 1 Thessalonians 1:4; 1 Peter 2:9, 10

The Case: *Why did God choose to love us?*

Simple Supplies: You'll need a Bible, scissors, and a box of playing cards. (The ace of hearts will be key in this object talk, but if you'd rather use Old Maid type cards, prepare your own card of the same size and draw a large red heart on it.) If you plan on doing the extra-time activity, you'll need white cotton fabric, fabric paints, a stapler, twigs, and twine.

Before class, cut a ¼-inch wide by 2-inch long slot on the back of the card box. This is the "push slot." Place the ace of hearts (or the card you've made) at the back of the card box and slide the rest of the cards into the box. Use your forefinger to practice sliding the ace of hearts upward from the back of the box so that the hearts show toward the audience. During the object talk, it will appear as if you've amazingly chosen this card from all of the others and caused it to rise above the rest! (Slick, isn't it?) The big hints: Always keep the ace of hearts in the back of the box so it will rise facing the kids. Never let kids see the back of the card box!

Discover 'n Do!

Be sure the "chosen card" is at the back of the box ready to rise and face your audience. Remove all of the other cards and quickly set the card box aside for now. Ask kids if they've ever been chosen for a special team, club, or project. Encourage kids to tell how it feels to be wanted and chosen. Then say: **Being chosen and specially wanted is a wonderful feeling; likewise, it's not a nice feeling to feel left out. I have something special to show you about being chosen and never left out again! We'll use these cards to help us.**

Have kids pass the cards around the table and place a card face down in front of themselves as they say their names. Then continue with the following poem:

So many people in different places,
So many hearts and smiling faces!
It may appear we're standing spread apart,
But God gathers us up and holds us to his heart! (gather up the cards)
He takes his chosen people and mixes us with love, (shuffle the cards)
Until we're all one body held together by God above! (place the cards in the box)
Doesn't it feel great to know God has set us apart?
We're God's chosen people—we're number ONE in his heart! (slide the ace of hearts upward)

Say: **Just as I chose the number one from all these cards, God chooses to set us apart for his love! But why did God choose us, and what does that mean in our lives? Let's see if we can solve the case with a little detective work and the Bible!**

Collect the Clues!

Form three small groups and assign each group one of these verses to read and discuss: Colossians 3:12; 1 Thessalonians 1:4; and 1 Peter 2:9, 10. Have groups visit about what their verses teach us about being chosen by God and how being chosen changes our lives in wonderful ways. Then come together as a group and share the discoveries and insights. Ask:

✔ **How does being chosen by God help us serve him? obey him? treat others with more kindness?**

✔ **In what ways does God show his love for us by choosing us to be his special people?**

✔ **How does living as God's chosen people draw us closer to God? strengthen our faith?**

Show kids how the card trick works, then challenge kids to try this neat trick at home as they remind their families of what it means to be chosen by God as his special people. If there's time, let kids use fabric paints to write "Chosen by God, chosen by love!" on squares of fabric. Staple the top and bottom of the each square of fabric to a long twig, then add a twine hanger.

Close by saying: **Good for you—you've solved the clues! God has chosen us to serve, obey, and follow him in special ways, and we can rejoice in being God's chosen people. This case is closed!**

RISE UP!

Psalms 17:6; 141:2; Proverbs 15:29; Jonah 2:7

The Case: *Does God really hear our prayers?*

Simple Supplies: You'll need a Bible, balloons, a plate, powdered unflavored gelatin, a wool sock, permanent markers, slips of paper, and pens.

Before class, practice this simple static electricity trick. Blow up and tie off a balloon and pour powdered gelatin in the center of a plate. Use a permanent marker to write the word "God" on the balloon. Rub the balloon for a minute with a wool sock to create static electricity. (Be sure the sock is wool! A wool mitten or piece of fabric will also work, but it must be wool.) Now hold the balloon slightly over the gelatin. The static charge will cause the gelatin to rise to the balloon! If the charge is great enough, the gelatin should create a "bridge" to the balloon. You'll be equating the rising gelatin to the way our prayers rise to God. Plan on having a balloon for each child to decorate with permanent markers. Hint: To create a strong static charge, rub one side of the balloon heavily and hold that side over the gelatin.

Discover 'n Do!

Be sure to have the gelatin poured in a pile in the center of a plate and a balloon blown up and ready to go. Gather kids and ask them to tell about things that rise through the air such as clouds, steam, hot-air balloons, and jet planes. As kids tell their ideas, pass the balloon and wool sock around the room and let kids take turns rubbing the sock against the balloon. Then as you rub the balloon a bit more with the wool, say: **Many things in our everyday world rise high, but nothing rises as high or as powerfully as the way our prayers rise to God each day! Let's see what I mean.** Point to the gelatin. **We can pretend these are the prayers we pray each day and this balloon will represent God. What happens to the prayers we pray? Does God really hear every prayer? Let's see if we can solve the case with a little detective work!**

Collect the Clues!

Rub the balloon a bit more, then say: **Do our prayers rise to God?** Hold the balloon over the gelatin and watch as the granules leap to the balloon.

Say: **They sure do! Our prayers rise quickly to God's ears and heart! God promises to hear and answer each of our prayers in his own time and way. How do we know? The Bible tells us so!** Have kids read aloud the following verses: Jonah 2:7; Psalms 17:6; 141:2; and Proverbs 15:29. Then ask:

✔ **Why do you think God wants to hear each of our prayers?**

✔ **In what ways does it help our faith to know that God hears all of our prayers?**

✔ **Why do you think God chooses to answer prayers in his own time and way?**

✔ **How does God show his love by hearing our prayers?**

Have kids write short prayers on slips of paper, then roll them up and slide them into balloons. Blow up and tie off the balloons, then have kids use permanent markers to write "Prayers have power to rise!" on their balloons. Challenge kids to hold their balloons each night they pray for the next week and to be aware of how God is answering them.

Show kids how this cool static trick was done, then tell kids to try this demonstration at home to remind others that our prayers rise to God. Close by saying: **Good for you—you've solved the clues! Because God loves and cares for us, he hears and answers every prayer in his time and way. This case is closed!**

BUBBLIN' OVER!

Deuteronomy 10:12, 13; Luke 4:8; Ephesians 6:7

The Case: *How does God help us serve?*

Simple Supplies: You'll need a Bible, a glass bowl, baking soda, white vinegar, and a tray or cookie sheet. If you plan on doing the extra-time activity, you'll also need water, permanent markers, and a small spray bottle for each child.

Before class, collect your materials for the object talk. You may want to measure out a quarter cup of baking soda into the glass bowl. During the presentation, you'll be pouring vinegar into the baking soda and causing the dry soda to "boil" and bubble over the sides of the bowl onto the tray or cookie sheet. If you plan on doing the extra-time craft activity, kids will be

making their own spray bottles of vinegar and water window cleaner to use in serving at home.

Discover 'n Do!

Place the glass bowl with the baking soda on a tray or cookie sheet. Have the bottle of vinegar handy. Say: **The powder in this bowl is dry and not active. It's just sitting there doing nothing. Too many times the dry powder is like our hearts when it comes to serving and helping others and God. We become dry and inactive and may just sit without serving. Maybe we don't think there's time to serve, or maybe we fool ourselves into thinking we're too young or don't have enough money. But God can help us serve him and others in amazing ways when he adds his wisdom, power, and love to the mix!**

Ask a volunteer to pour a portion of the vinegar into the bowl until the mixture bubbles over the top of the bowl. (It will take about a half cup of vinegar.) As the mixture bubbles and becomes "alive," say: **Wow! God's wisdom, power, and love really make our hearts overflow with love and the desire to serve and help! But what does God's love do for us, and what are ways he tells us to serve? Let's see if we can solve the case with a little detective work and the Bible!**

Collect the Clues!

Have kids form small groups to discover the answers to the following Who, What, Why, and How questions. Ask the following questions, then have groups look up the references, read them aloud, and briefly discuss the answer to each question. Have kids share their discoveries with the entire group.

> ✔ *WHO are we to serve and WHY?* (Luke 4:8)
> ✔ *WHAT five things does God command us to do?* (Deuteronomy 10:12, 13)
> ✔ *HOW are we to serve God and others?* (Romans 1:9; Galatians 5:13b; and Ephesians 6:7)

After reading and discussing the answers, ask:
> ✔ **Why are we to serve only God, and through him other people?**
> ✔ **How does loving God help us serve him?**
> ✔ **In what ways do God's wisdom, power, and love help us serve?**

Say: **When we know God's wisdom, power, and love are with us, our hearts bubble over with love and the desire to serve! And we**

don't have to worry about the details of who or how to serve because God will help us! We just need to be ready and willing to bubble over with love and joy in serving! Close by saying: **Good for you—you've solved the clues! God helps us serve through our time, talents, money, and love. The case is closed!** Show kids how to make the bowl bubble over if you desire. Tell them this is an easy trick to show at home as they remind others about the ways God helps us serve.

If there's time, let kids use permanent markers to decorate plastic spray bottles. Then mix one part vinegar to six parts water in each bottle. Challenge kids to use their spray cleaners to serve at home by cleaning windows, appliances, sinks, and even spills on tile floors.

(G)OD'S BANDAGE

Psalms 30:2; 103:2-5; 147:3; Romans 5:5

The Case: *How does God heal our broken hearts?*

Simple Supplies: You'll need a Bible, a push pin, red paper or vinyl tape, a dish pan or large bowl, and a plastic soda-pop bottle with a screw-on top. (If you plan on practicing this trick, you'll need two plastic bottles—one for practice and one for the object talk.)

Before class, prepare and practice this slick trick. Make a red heart shape on the front of the plastic bottle using either red vinyl electrical tape or red paper. Fill the bottle with water. During the object talk, you'll be pushing a push pin into the lower half of the bottle. When the bottle top is removed, the bottle will leak liquid into the pan or bowl. When the top is replace tightly, the flow will stop! Try this with your practice bottle and push pin over a sink. The big hint: Be careful not to squeeze the bottle during the object talk.

Discover 'n Do!

Be sure the bottle is filled with water. Set the dish pan or bowl and push pin beside the bottle. Invite kids to tell about times they felt hurt, brokenhearted, or discouraged and sad. Encourage them to tell what they did to feel better. Then hold up the bottle with the heart and say: **Let's pretend this bottle represents our hearts and the water is the love inside. When troubles and hurts come along and poke at our hearts** (poke the push pin into the bottle toward the bottom, remove the bottle cap, and let the water drip into the pan), **it's hard not to let our love seep away little by little. Discouragement, sadness, hurts, and heartache may drain away our ability to be kind and loving. So what can stop the hurt and fill us again? God's love and protection!**

Screw the bottle top on tightly. **God wipes away our tears and heals our hurts so our love doesn't leak away even though there may still be troubles poking at us!** Wipe any drips from the bottle, which should now have stopped leaking even though there is a hole in the bottle. (Amazing, isn't it?) **But how does God heal our hearts, and how does he refill our hearts continually with love? Let's see if we can solve the case with a little detective work and the Bible!** Set the bottle in the dish pan or bowl.

Collect the Clues!

Have kids read aloud Psalm 103:2-5 and identify all the things God does for us (forgives our sins, heals diseases, redeems our lives, crowns us with love, and satisfies our desires). Ask:

✔ **How does God doing all these things for us heal our hurt feelings and heartaches?**

✔ **In what ways do forgiveness, redemption, love, and answering our needs fill us with love?**

Read aloud Psalms 30:2 and 147:3. Then ask:

✔ **Why do you think God wants to heal and help us?**

✔ **How is God's healing a demonstration of his love for us?**

Read aloud Romans 5:5, then ask:

✔ **How does God fill our hearts continually with more love?**

✔ **In what ways does healing by God and being filled with love from the Holy Spirit help us serve God? help strengthen our faith? help us through more hard times?**

Pour more water into the bottle and say: **God heals our hurts and fills our hearts with love through the Holy Spirit every day so we never have to worry about our love leaking away!** Remove the bottle top again for a moment and say: **When our hearts feel as if they're losing love and kindness** (replace the bottle top to stop the leaking), **God stops the hurts and fills us with lasting love!** Close by saying: **Good for you—**

you've solved the clues! God heals our hurts through his powerful love. The case is closed!

If there's time, let kids make posters to remind them that God heals our hearts. For each poster, have kids write the word "HEAL" in the centers of construction paper using plastic bandages to form the uppercase letters. Then write "God will" just above the word "HEAL" and the words "us. Psalm 147:3" below so the poster reads: "God will HEAL us. Psalm 147:3."

(H)IDDEN HEARTS?

Psalm 139:23, 24; Proverbs 16:23; Matthew 15:18

The Case: *Can we hide our thoughts from God?*

Simple Supplies: You'll need a Bible, two clear drinking glasses (smooth sided), red construction paper, scissors, water, and markers or pens. If you plan to do the extra-time activity, you'll need a clear plastic glass for each child.

Before class, practice this neat demonstration. Cut two red paper hearts that will fit under the bottoms of the clear drinking glasses you'll be using. On one heart, write a negative word such as hate, envy, *or* greed. *On the other heart, write a positive word such as* love, faith, *or* truth. *Now place the glasses filled with water over the hearts. When you look through the sides of the glasses, you won't be able to see the hearts. But look down through the water and you can read the hearts! You'll be showing kids how impossible it is to hide the condition of our hearts from God even though we think it's hidden.*

Discover 'n Do!

Before the object talk, place the drinking glasses full of water over the two hearts. Ask kids if they've ever played the game of Hide-n-Seek. Say: **It's fun to play Hide-n-Seek, isn't it? Sometimes we even play Hide-n-Seek with the feelings and thoughts that are in our hearts. Maybe we're angry or hurt and don't want others to know it. We hide away our hearts and the feelings inside. Look through the sides of these glasses.** Pause while kids look *through* the glass, then continue: **There are hearts hidden inside, but we can't see them. This is what it's like** when we try to hide our feelings and thoughts from others. But can we hide our hearts from God? Look down *into* the glasses—what do you see now?

Have kids peer through the tops of the glasses and read the words on the hearts. **God sees the good and bad things that live in our hearts. But how do our feelings and thoughts affect the ways we live and honor God? Let's see if we can solve the case with a little detective work and the Bible!**

Collect the Clues!

Have volunteers read the following verses: Psalm 139:1, 2, 23, 24; Proverbs 16:23; 17:20; 27:19; and Matthew 15:18. Then ask:

- ✔ **How does the fact that God created us allow him to know our thoughts and feelings?**
- ✔ **In what ways do our thoughts, feelings, and attitudes of the heart come out in our words and actions?**
- ✔ **Why is it important to keep good, positive thoughts and feelings in our hearts?**

Say: **We might try to hide feelings and thoughts from others, and maybe we can for awhile. But we can't hide from God! God created us and knows every thought and feeling we may try to hide from him. And God knows what is in our hearts will come out in our words and actions. That's why it's important to keep good thoughts and feelings inside us.**

Close by saying: **Good for you—you've solved the clues! God knows our every thought and sees inside our hearts. And God wants us to keep good thoughts and feelings in our hearts so they come out in our words and actions. This case is closed!**

If there is enough time, hand each child a clear plastic cup. Have kids cut out paper hearts to fit under the cups and then write positive words such as *love, hope, truth,* and *kindness* on the hearts. Challenge kids to present this neat now-you-see-it, now-you-don't demonstration to friends and family members as they remind others that God knows what is in our hearts.

HOLD TIGHT!

Psalm 37:3, 5; Proverbs 3:5, 6; Isaiah 12:2

The Case: *How can we hold on to God?*

Simple Supplies: You'll need a Bible, thick rope, modeling clay or florists' clay, spray paint or self-adhesive shelf paper, scissors, and a plastic soda-pop bottle. If you plan on doing the extra-time activity, you'll need the following for each child: a painted plastic soda-pop bottle, modeling dough, and an 8-inch piece of thick rope.

Before class, spray paint a plastic soda-pop bottle or cover the bottle with self-adhesive paper so kids can't see inside the bottle. (Prepare painted bottles for kids if you plan to do the extra-time craft.) Roll a ball of clay or clay large enough to push into the bottle, then cut an 8-inch piece of thick rope.

During the object talk, you'll show the bottle and rope (but not the hidden dough ball!), turn the bottle upside down, and poke the rope into the bottle. The rope will hang by itself. Next, you'll quickly lift up the rope and the bottle will hang miraculously from the rope without falling! (The dough ball will be stuck in the neck of the bottle and hold the rope from slipping out!)

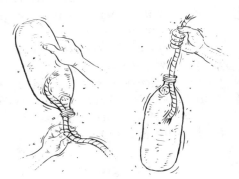

Discover 'n Do!

Have the bottle with the hidden clay on a table, but don't let kids inspect the bottle. Set the rope beside the bottle. Ask kids to tell what things they trust in, such as their parents, the sunrise, or that their friends will be there for them when needed. Then say: **We often place our trust in many people and things, but not everyone or all things are trustworthy! I have a rope and a bottle here. If I hold the bottle upside down like this** (turn the bottle upside down being careful not to "clunk" the dough ball) **and if I push the rope into the end, we can trust the rope probably to stay put, right?** (Hold the bottle and rope nearly upside down letting the rope swing free.) **What can you trust to happen if I hold the bottle by the rope?** Pause for kids to say that the bottle will fall, then grab the rope and hold on to the end as the bottle "miraculously" hangs in place. Say: **Wow!**

What we trusted would happen didn't happen after all! The bottle is clinging to the rope in an awesome way that may not even make sense. This is how God wants us to hold on to him—radically and awesomely! God wants us to trust in him and cling to him in amazing ways even during the toughest times. But how can we hold on to God in amazing ways, and what part does trust play in helping us hold on? Let's see if we can solve this case with a little detective work and the Bible! Set the bottle right-side up on the table and remove the rope.

Collect the Clues!

Form three groups and assign each group one of the following verses to read and discuss in the groups: Psalm 37:3, 5; Proverbs 3:5, 6; Isaiah 12:2. Have kids answer these questions: *How does trust help us hang on to God? What good things come from trusting God?* After kids are done discussing the verses, read each verse aloud and have groups share their discoveries. Then read aloud Psalm 25:5 and ask:

✔ **In what ways does trust lead to hope?**

✔ **Why is it important to have hope and trust?**

✔ **Why is God the only solid place to put our hope?**

Say: **Trusting in people and earthly things or hanging on to things such as money or possessions isn't wise** (place the rope in the right-side up bottle and lift it using your fingers, then let the bottle drop onto the table) **because we'll be let down in many ways! But when we trust in and hang on to God** (turn the bottle upside down and place the rope into the bottle, then pick up the end of the rope and let the bottle swing from the rope), **he will keep us from falling!** Close by saying: **Good for you— you've solved the clues! By placing our trust in God, we'll be able to hang on in the toughest times or situations. This case is closed!**

If there's time, show kids how the trick works, then let them make their own amazing "hang-on" bottles. Give each child a painted plastic pop bottle, a lump of clay, and an 8-inch piece of thick rope. Show kids how the trick works, then let them assemble their projects and practice presenting the object talk to partners. Challenge kids to present the object talk at home as they remind their families and friends about the importance of hanging on to God through trust and hope.

YOU'RE A POSSIBILITY!

Matthew 19:26; Mark 10:27; Luke 1:37; John 15:5

The Case: *What can I do with God's help?*

Simple Supplies: You'll need a Bible, construction paper, scissors, tape, and markers. If you do the extra-time activity, you'll also want additional construction paper, glitter glue, and scissors.

Before class, cut a large, thick letter P from construction paper. Make sure the letter is large enough to write on. Tape the letter to a wall or chalkboard and keep markers nearby. Try this simple trick with a friend or family member to get the hang of it. Hold both of your arms in front of you. Bend your elbows in so that your forearms go across your body, then touch the tips of your forefingers together and hold them there. Have another person grasp your wrists and steadily try to pull your fingers apart. It can't be done! Kids will be doing this neat demonstration in pairs.

Discover 'n Do!

Invite kids to name various things that they believe are impossible or very difficult for them (or any other person to do). Suggestions might range from moving mountains to getting a perfect score on a spelling test to scoring the winning goal in a championship soccer game. Say: **Here's something that seems very possible to do but may not be as easy as it looks!** Have kids get with partners or trios and instruct them to take turns being the fingertip holders and the pullers as you direct them how to hold their fingertips and how to try pulling them apart. Be sure each child has a turn to be the holder and the puller.

Then say: **Wow! This isn't as possible as it seems, is it? That's the way it is with many things in our lives. We may think we can't do something because we're too young, too short, too weak, too poor, or too busy. Just think of how many times we give those excuses. What we're really saying is, "I don't trust God to help me." But can God really help us do anything he wants us to do? Does God really have the power to turn every impossibility into a possibility with a capital P?** Point to the large letter P on the wall. **Let's see if we can solve this case with a little detective work and the Bible!**

Collect the Clues!

Have kids form four small groups and hand each group a marker. Have each group look up and read one of the following verses: Matthew 19:26; Mark 10:27; Luke 1:37; and John 15:5. Instruct kids to read the verses aloud in their groups, then decide if the verse tells us that God can do anything and so can we through God. If they think the verse says God can do anything, have groups draw an up arrow on the letter P. If they think their verse says God can't do all things, have them draw a down arrow. (All of the arrows should point upward!)

When all the arrows have been drawn, ask:

✔ **Why do you think it is possible for God to turn all things into possibilities?**

✔ **In what ways can we become possibilities for God?**

✔ **How does knowing God helps us accomplish all things in his plans give us confidence to do God's work?**

✔ **Why does it strengthen our faith to know that with God all things are possible?**

Say: **With God, all things *are* possible. And through God's powerful help, we become possibilities with a capital P! We can serve in every way, we can tell others about the Lord, and we can accomplish all God wants us to. And we never have to worry about being too small, too young, too busy, or too anything! We're possibilities with a capital P!**

If you know the words to the song "I Am a Possibility," lead kids in singing through the song. Then close by saying: **Good for you—you've solved the clues! Now we all know that God turns every impossibility into a wonderful possibility and even into a probability. This case is closed!**

If there's extra time, let kids embellish large letter P's made from colorful construction paper. Use markers and glitter glue to write Luke 1:37 on the letters ("For nothing is impossible with God"). Have kids present this object talk to their families and friends to remind them that we're all possibilities when we trust God!

ALWAYS NEAR

Deuteronomy 31:6; Joshua 1:9; Psalms 1:6; 139:7-10

The Case: *Does God ever leave us?*

Simple Supplies: You'll need a Bible, a men's handkerchief, tacky craft glue, and flat toothpicks. If you plan on letting kids make their own object-talk props, plan on having a handkerchief or 12-inch square of fabric for each child plus extra toothpicks.

Before class, prepare and practice this nifty sleight-of-hand trick. You'll be making it seem as if a toothpick is disappearing and reappearing at will. Using tacky craft glue, make a small hem along one side of the handkerchief to make a secret pocket. (The hem needs to be just wide enough to slip a toothpick into.) Allow the glue to dry, then slip a toothpick into the secret pocket. During the object talk, you'll hold up the second toothpick so kids can see it, then wrap it slyly in the handkerchief, folding it a bit in the fabric and holding it with your thumb so it doesn't fall out. This will make the toothpick seem to disappear. You'll have kids feel the hidden toothpick and think it's in place before you unfold the handkerchief and no tooth-pick is seen! To make the toothpick "reappear," simply fold up the handkerchief again and secretly unfurl the toothpick you were holding against your thumb. Kids will be amazed!

Discover 'n Do!

Have one of the toothpicks already hidden in the secret pocket of the handkerchief. Then hold up the handkerchief and the other toothpick. Say: **Let's pretend this toothpick represents God in our lives. By faith and trust we know that God is present and working in our lives. But some-times we go through tough times that seem to cover up our faith.** (Cover the toothpick and hide it in fabric against your thumb.) **We may not see what God is doing or get answers to our prayers right away. We want to be assured God is still with us.** (Let kids feel the toothpick in the hidden pocket. They'll think it is the toothpick you just covered up.)

But when times are really tough and situations are sad or frustrating, we may worry and think, "God has left me! I think he has disappeared!" (Unfold the handkerchief and hold it up to look as though the toothpick has disappeared.) **But does God ever decide to leave us when the going is rough? Does God truly stay with us even when our faith wobbles? Let's see if we can solve this case with a little detective work and the Bible!** Continue holding the toothpick for a few minutes as you read the verses in the next section.

Collect the Clues!

Read aloud Deuteronomy 31:6 and Joshua 1:9, then say: **Wow! God made us a special promise never to leave us! So no matter how tough the going gets, God is still with us and at work in our lives!** (Crumple up the handkerchief, then unfurl it to reveal the toothpick you've been holding against your thumb.) Hold up the toothpick and say: **God never leaves us even for a moment. Let's see what else God's Word tells us about God's continual presence.** Set aside the toothpick and handkerchief.

Have volunteers read aloud Psalms 1:6 and 139:7-10. Then ask:

✔ **Why do you think God wants to stay with us all the time?**
✔ **Are there times we turn our backs on God? What do you think God does then?**
✔ **How does God's presence show his love for us?**
✔ **How does knowing God never leaves you help when you face tough times?**

Say: **We all wonder at times if God is still with us and listening to our prayers. That's human nature. But with divine faith we can be assured that God never leaves us and is always working in our lives. We may not understand how God is working, or we may think our timetable is better than God's, but our job is to trust God and know he is with us at all times!** Close by saying: **Good for you—you've solved the clues! God never leaves us and is always at work in our lives—day and night forever. This case is closed!**

If there's time, show kids how you did the disappearing-reappearing toothpick trick. Then hand kids the handkerchiefs and show them how to glue the tiny hems. When the handkerchiefs are dry, distribute two toothpicks to each child and let kids practice the object talk. Challenge kids to show their object talks to others as they remind their families and friends about God's continual presence in our lives.

KNOWING THE FUTURE

Ecclesiastes 3:1, 14; 7:14; Jeremiah 10:12, 13; 29:11

The Case: *Is it possible to know the future?*

Simple Supplies: You'll need a Bible, paper, pens, and tape. If you plan on doing the extra-time craft activity, you'll need a clear glass or plastic Christmas ball for each child plus paint pens, glitter, scissors, and empty egg cartons. (Note: This object talk involves adding and subtracting three-digit numbers, so it's best suited for kids in third grade and above.)

Before class, write the numeral "1,089" on a sheet of paper. You'll have this paper taped face down to the wall or chalkboard. Kids will add and subtract a series of numbers, and all the kids will arrive at the very same answer—which is 1,089—no matter what numbers they were calculating! (Awesome, isn't it?) You'll appear to be able to predict the future with this cool trick.

Discover 'n Do!

Before class, be sure you have the paper with 1,089 written on it taped face down to the wall or a chalkboard. Distribute paper and pens to the kids, then tell kids they'll be playing a number game with adding and subtracting numbers. Tell kids you have an amazing ability to predict the exact answer each of them will have at the end of the number game. Ask kids if they think it's possible for you to know, in advance, what answer each person will have. Then give the following series of instructions. (Samples are given in the righthand column, but any numbers will work if kids follow the instructions!)

1. Write down any 3-digit number in which
   the first and last digits differ by at least two: 481
2. Write the reverse of this number: 184
3. Subtract the smaller from the larger: 297
4. Write the reverse of this number: 792
5. Add the two numbers together: 1,089

As kids follow the directions, tell them to keep their papers covered so no one sees their answers! When you've finished, say: **To prove I can**

predict your answers, I've written a number on this paper. If this is your answer, stand up. Turn over the paper to reveal the number. If kids did their math correctly, they should all have the very same number and be standing!

Say: **Wow! You didn't think I could know your answers before you figured them, did you? And each of you began with different numbers. Well, of course I had to use a trick to accomplish this feat of telling the future. But there is someone who knows the answers to all life's questions and who can predict the future because he controls everything! Who do you think I'm talking about?** Pause for responses, then ask: **Is it possible for us to know the future? How does God know the future? Let's see if we can solve this case with a little detective work and the Bible!**

Collect the Clues!

Have volunteers read aloud Ecclesiastes 3:1, 14; 7:14; 8:7; Jeremiah 10:12, 13; 29:11; and Job 37:15-18. Then ask:

✔ **How did God's creation of the world let him know the future?**
✔ **If God knows the future, why is it important to know God's Word?**
✔ **What does God promise in the future if we know, love, and follow him?**
✔ **How can trusting that God is already in the future give us hope for today?**

Say: **God created the world and controls all things, including the future. We may not be able to tell exactly what will happen tomorrow or in a hundred years, but we do know one thing: God is already in the future, and he is in control! When we choose to know, love, and follow God in all we do and say, we can hope in tomorrow and know our future will be loving and bright! Is it possible to tell the future? Only through trusting God and accepting his control. This case is closed!**

If there's time, hand each child a cup from a cut-apart egg carton and a clear glass or plastic Christmas ornament. Tell kids that crystal balls are phony—that only God can tell the future—but that these special ornaments will remind them that God has control over the future because he has created it. Have kids use paint pens to write "Our future is in God!" on the balls, then decorate the balls any way they choose. Set the balls in the egg cups to dry.

WORD OF WONDER!

Deuteronomy 4:10; Psalm 119:11; 2 Timothy 3:16, 17

The Case: *Why should we learn Scripture?*

Simple Supplies: You'll need a Bible, white copy paper, cotton swabs, lemon juice, markers, tape, and a lamp with a light bulb (no shade). If you plan on kids doing the extra-time activity, have extra paper, cotton swabs, and cups of lemon juice.

Before class, try this neat demonstration at home. Use cotton swabs and lemon juice to write "God's Word is alive!" on a sheet of white copy paper. Let the paper dry, and the message should be invisible. Remove the shade from a lamp with an incandescent bulb and hold the paper several inches above the bulb. Move the paper back and forth across the bulb until the message begins to appear. The lemon juice will turn brown from the heat of the bulb, revealing the hidden message! For class, prepare another page identical to the one you just practiced with. Kids will be making secret-message papers to take home and show their families and friends.

Discover 'n Do!

Have the lamp (minus the shade) set up and ready to be turned on. Place the paper with the secret message beside the lamp. Read aloud Psalm 119:105, then ask kids to tell how God's Word is like a bright lamp or light in our lives. Turn on the lamp and say: **God's Word is also called** *Scripture,* **and it is filled with truth and wisdom to help us learn to live as God desires.** Hold up the white paper and say: **This paper has an important hidden message about Scripture. We'll take turns moving it across the light and see what happens.** As you speak, take turns passing the paper over the bulb. Say: **Scripture lights our hearts and minds and shines the light on God's truth. It lights the way for us to go through life so we don't fall into lies and other traps. And just as light chases away darkness, God's Word chases away the darkness of evil!**

Have kids name other ways that light is like God's Word. Suggestions might include that light gives warmth just as God's Word gives warmth and comfort. When the message is visible, read it aloud and ask kids in what ways Scripture is alive. Then say: **We've seen what the secret mes-sage is and how God's Word is like warmth and light. But why**

should we take the time to learn Scripture? How can it help us live as God desires? Let's see if we can solve this case with a little detective work and the Bible!

Collect the Clues!

Tape the secret-message sheet to the wall or a door and place markers nearby. As kids read aloud 2 Timothy 3:16 and 17, have them list on the paper the ways God's Word helps us or what it is useful for. Then invite volunteers to read aloud Deuteronomy 4:10 and Psalm 119:11, 65, 66, and 69. Ask:

✔ **Why is it wise to read and learn what God says?**
✔ **How does learning, understanding, and using Scripture show God that we love him? that we appreciate all he teaches us?**
✔ **How can learning God's Word bring us closer to him?**

Say: **We can choose to spend time in many ways. We can listen to music, watch television, play with friends, participate in sports, and even paint pictures. But one of the best ways to spend time is in learning God's Word. If we spend time each day picking out a verse and trying to learn it by heart, just think how pleased God will be! God gave us his Word to learn and use in our lives each day—and that's no secret message!** Close by saying: **Good for you—you've solved the clues! It's important to learn God's Word to live as God desires us to live and so we draw closer to God and his truth! This case is closed!**

If there's time, show kids how this demonstration was done. Have kids use lemon juice to write "God's Word is alive!" on white paper to take home and show their families and friends as they remind them about the importance of learning Scripture.

# POWER IN PRAYER

Psalm 17:6; Isaiah 58:9; Acts 12:4-14; James 5:16

The Case: *What real power is in prayer?*

Simple Supplies: You'll need a Bible, a plastic cup, a dime, a handkerchief, scissors, and a rubber band. If you plan on doing the extra-

time craft activity, you'll need paper towels, rubber bands, permanent markers, and a plastic cup for each child. (If you desire, have a dime for each child.)

Before class, prepare and practice this slick trick. To prepare the plastic cup, cut a thin slot near the bottom of the cup using scissors or a box cutter. Make the slit large enough for a dime to barely slide through. (Be sure not to let kids see the slit in the cup!) During the object talk, you'll place a dime in the cup and cover the top with a handkerchief and rubber band. As you talk, you'll gently shake the cup and the dime will slide through the slit into your hand. As kids focus their attention on the cup, you'll switch hands with the cup and secretly hide the dime in your hand. Then after kids see the dime has amazingly escaped, you'll produce the coin in your hand! (Simply astounding, isn't it?) Practice the story presentation below along with the accompanying actions to make your presentation smooth.

Discover 'n Do!

Have the cup, dime, rubber band, and handkerchief handy. (Remember not to let kids see the slit in the cup). Gather kids and tell them you have an amazing Bible story to tell them that involves the power of prayer. Explain that the dime represents Peter and the cup, his jail cell. Tell the following story from Acts 12:4-14 as you perform the accompanying actions with the cup and coin.

Peter had been telling others about Jesus and his saving love. The authorities were angry and tossed Peter in a prison cell. (Place the dime in the cup.) **Two guards stood watch over Peter as he prayed. Peter asked God to help him. Peter prayed, and so did his friends. Did God hear them? You bet he did! Peter and the guards fell asleep. Let's cover them up.** (Cover the cup with the handkerchief.) **There Peter slept between the guards with his hands and feet in chains!** (Place the rubber band around the top of the cup.) **Suddenly an angel appeared and gently shook Peter awake.** (Gently shake the coin into your hand. As you continue talking, keep kids focusing on the cup as you switch hands and secretly hold the dime in the hand without the cup.) **"Peter! Follow me!" said the angel—and Peter followed the angel.** (Transfer the cup to your other hand and move it along as if it's walking.) **Did Peter and the angel escape jail and get to safety? Let's see!** (Uncover the cup, being careful not to let kids see the slit in the cup or the dime hidden in your hand.) **Peter had escaped! The power of prayer worked!**

Where did Peter go? (Reveal the coin in your other hand.) **Peter went to his friends so they could praise God together!** (Hold the coin high.)

Wow! That was an exciting story, wasn't it? What power is waiting for us in prayer? Let's see if we can solve the case with a little detective work and the Bible!

Collect the Clues!

Set the cup and dime aside. Invite volunteers to read aloud the following verses. When kids hear something that tells about the power of prayer, have them jump up and shout, "There's real power in prayer!" Read Isaiah 58:9a; Psalm 17:6; and James 5:16b. Then ask:

- ✔ **How does God reveal his power through our prayers? his love? his wisdom?**
- ✔ **Why is it wise to pray continually?**
- ✔ **In what ways does praying for others help them? help us? honor God?**
- ✔ **How does praying to God demonstrate our faith in him? show our love?**

Say: **There is real power in praying to God. He promises to hear our prayers and to answer them in his own time and way. And praying for others is a powerful way to give them our help and love!** Close by saying: **Good for you—you've solved the clues! There is real power in prayer, and we can put that power to use every day we pray. This case is closed!**

If there's time, show kids how you made the coin disappear and reappear. Then let kids make their own cups with slits. Tell kids to use permanent markers to write "There's power in prayer!" on the cups. Then distribute rubber bands and paper towels to use as covers for the cups. Tell kids to use dimes during their presentations as they retell the story of Peter's powerful prayer.

GOD'S MATH

Proverbs 21:26; Matthew 10:8; 2 Corinthians 9:6-12

The Case: *Why should we give to others?*

Simple Supplies: You'll need a Bible, six pennies, sticky tack or chewing gum, and a table. If you plan on doing the extra-time craft activity, you'll also need small plastic pop bottles and lids, scissors, glue and water, cotton swabs, and colorful tissue paper.

Before class, practice the slick trick to make your presentation smooth during class. Stick three pennies under the edge of a table with a tiny bit of sticky tack or chewed chewing gum. Place three pennies in your hand. During the object talk, you'll slide the pennies on the table into your hand as you count them aloud—and slyly add a penny at a time from under the table to your hand. You'll repeat the object talk three times until you're holding six pennies in all! It will appear as if the pennies are mysteriously appearing in your hand. For the extra-time craft activity, cut slits in the sides of the plastic pop bottles for coins to slide through. Mix white craft glue with a bit of water to make it thin. Kids will brush glue over tissue paper in mosaic style to cover their bottles and make nifty coin banks.

Discover 'n Do!

Be sure the pennies are in place before kids arrive for class. When you're ready for the object talk, show kids the three pennies in your hand. Ask them what they could do with three pennies. Then say: **Three pennies may not seem like much, but they can multiply in wonderful ways through God's blessings! I will count these pennies into my hand as you say, "Two times two is four, but God can multiply much, much more!**"

Have kids repeat this rhyme a couple of times, then slide the pennies into your hand as kids repeat the rhyme. Quickly add a penny from under the table to your hand, then place the pennies on the table and count them aloud. Continue in the same way until you count six pennies on the table. Say: **Wow! God multiplies blessings into many more than he started with. But why should we share with others? Why should we give to others from the blessings God gives us? Let's see if we can solve the case with a little detective work and the Bible!**

Collect the Clues!

Have kids take turns reading verses from Proverbs 21:26b; Matthew 10:8b; and 2 Corinthians 9:6-12. Then ask:

✔ **What does God teach us about giving to others and sharing?**

✔ **What does God promise will happen if we share with others?**

✔ **How can our blessings be multiplied when we give to other people who are in need?**

✔ **What are ways we can give to and share with others?**

Say: **God promises that if we give to others and share with cheerful hearts, he will multiply our blessings even more. That's a powerful and wonderful promise, isn't it? God has blessed each of us with wonderful things such as good homes, good food, and nice clothes. We can share those nice things with people who may not have all we have. And we never have to feel like we won't have enough because God promises to multiply our blessings even more when we give and share. Now that's what I call God's awesome math!**

Close by saying: **Good for you—you've solved the clues! We can give to and share with others out of the blessings God gives us. And when we do, God will bless us even more! This case is closed!**

If there's time, let kids make colorful banks by tearing pieces of bright tissue paper and using cotton swabs to brush the tissue onto plastic pop bottles. When the banks are dry, challenge kids to collect coins and watch them multiply into a whole bottle-full to give to someone in need!

CASE CLOSED!

SHOW 'N TELL CARDS

"For I know the plans I have for you," declares the Lord, "plans to prosper you and not to harm you, plans to give you hope and a future."
(Jeremiah 29:11)

And we know that in all things God works for the good of those who love him, who have been called according to his purpose.
(Romans 8:28)

For it is God who works in you to will and to act according to his good purpose.
(Philippians 2:13)

But the plans of the LORD stand firm forever, the purposes of his heart through all generations.
(Psalm 33:11)